ONCE YOU'RE INSIDE

POEMS EXPLORING INCARCERATION

by Ann Bracken

Praise for *Once You're Inside*

Language liberates. Ann Bracken, working as a poet/teacher, shines light into darkness so that prisoners become people of purpose who speak and are heard. Social action, at its truest meaning, reinforces the best in us, and Bracken takes charge in a journey of change not only for prisoners but for herself. The student-prisoners now know what it is to exist with a good practice. At the same time Bracken is writing her owns poems as commentaries. When poetic will and societal issues come together, we have a meaningful book; when lyricism and heart come together, we have a work of art.
Grace Cavalieri
Maryland Poet Laureate

In a collection of unflinching, gutsy, and heart-felt poems, *Once You're Inside* transports readers to the grim and grisly realities of America's prison industrial complex. Ann Bracken brilliantly inspires readers to explore both discomfort and shared humanity with renderings of life inside one of the most dehumanizing institutions in the modern world.
Jess Fletcher
Operations Director, Iron City Magazine

In *Once You're Inside*, Ann Bracken exposes the hidden infrastructure of prison and explores the interior lives of incarcerated men and women with tenderness and objectivity. Her artist's eye registers seemingly insignificant details that speak volumes about the myriad ways the carceral system attempts to rip away possibility, dignity, and human connection. Set within the most barren of landscapes, her poems convey the power of creative expression and shared stories that enables the human spirit to prevail.
Wendy Jason
Founding Director, Justice Arts Coalition

Ann Bracken's poetry collection, *Once You're Inside*, is jammed with meaningful vignettes about people in prison. Without being the least bit sentimental, she gives the reader insight into the minds and feelings of a wide range of incarcerated people—real people we can almost know from her poems. Each poem stands well alone, but read the entire book for a truthful portrayal of what life in prison is like.
Laura Bates, Associate Professor of English, Indiana State University
Author of *Shakespeare Saved My Life: Ten Years in Solitary with the Bard*

Once You're Inside:
Poems Exploring Incarceration

Ann Bracken

Charing Cross Press

Charing Cross Press
Simpsonville, MD

Copyright © 2022 by Ann Bracken

Charing Cross Press
Charing Cross Press

All rights reserved. No part of this book may be reproduced or transmitted in any other form or by any means, electronic or mechanical, including photocopying, recording, or by any information storage and retrieval system.

Printed in the United States of America

Library of Congress Control Number: 2021903174
ISBN 978-0-578-86768-7 Paperback

Cover design: Christine Rains
Cover art: Carole Alden
Book design: David Saunier
Logo design: Christella Potts
Photo credit: Brian Potts

DEDICATION

For the men and women incarcerated in the United States
and for their families
In grateful appreciation for all who shared their stories with me

"We are all broken by something. We have all hurt someone and have been hurt. We all share the condition of brokenness even if our brokenness is not equivalent....Each of us is more than the worst thing we've ever done."
~ *Bryan Stevenson*

ACKNOWLEDGMENTS

Fledgling Rag #18: "Between Here and Hope", "Nathaniel Breaks It Down for You", "Real for Real"

Gargoyle, "The Mental Health Box"

New Verse News, "$1 a Day to Fight the Largest Fire in California History"

The Skinny Poetry Journal, "On Walking by the Schoolyard"

Fourth River Press, "Dress Code for the Women's Prison"

Everyday Poems, "The Code"

Evening Street, "Paint Chips of Memory"

Maryland Writer's Association Poetry Anthology, "The Prisons on Constitution Street"

Iron City Magazine, "Sandbags Against the Flood," "Surviving the Lake in the Basement," "Lock Me Up"

TABLE OF CONTENTS

Dedication	5
Acknowledgments	6
Preface	10
Artist's Statement	14
Fence	15
The Code	16
Passage to Possibility	17
Transmute	18
Lock Me Up	19
What I Think About	20
She Literally Worked Herself to Death	21
Surviving the Lake in the Basement	22
$1 an Hour to Fight Largest Fire in California	23
Information Bulletin: Book Orders	24
Sandbags Against the Flood	25
Paint Chips of Memory: Baltimore Burning 1968 and 2015	26
A Visit to Constitution Street	27
Dress Code for the Women's Prison	29
Elevator Rules	30
In Need of a Phone	31
I'm Not Looking for Mercy	32
Walking by the School Yard	33
Flowers in Prison	34
Lodestars in the Basement	35
Maintenance	37
My Sister Brought Me a Gift (JC Speaks About His Work)	38
Letter from a Baltimore Jail	39
Nathaniel Breaks It Down for Me	40
No Sugar Inside	41

Parking Lot Rendezvous	42
Privilege	43
Real for Real	44
JC Sits in Solitary	45
Richard Sturn's Rules for Participation	46
Saved by Kindness	47
Saying Goodbye	48
The Literary Day of the Arts	49
The Mental Health Box	50
Hope on Hold	51
The Women's Prison	52
Visiting Room	53
Where's Mitch?	54
What They Need	55
Sessions with Rodrigo	56
I: Rodrigo	56
II: Writing Teacher	57

PREFACE

In 2015, my editor at *Little Patuxent Review*, a Maryland literary journal, gave me an assignment I wanted to refuse; she asked me to interview a professor who ran a prison-based writing group and then to visit the prison and interview the men. The woman who ran the group—Professor M., a sociology professor at a major research institution who'd volunteered in the prison for seven years, spoke very positively about the men in her group. Intrigued by all that she'd shared, but still frightened to go into a prison, my mind buzzed with all of the common middle-class stereotypes about "those people" behind bars. "Those people": school drop-outs, drug-dealers, hustlers, maybe even murderers. Despite the positive experiences of several of my writing colleagues, I'd kept my distance-- partly out of fear and partly because my protective shell had begun to crack as I learned more about the prison-industrial complex and the school-to-prison pipeline. Many of my former high-school students had brushes with the juvenile justice system, but none of them were especially "bad" kids. Instead, they were kids who had tough home-lives or who had made really poor, impulsive decisions that landed them in the lap of the law. Deep down my spirit realized that if I were to go into a prison and meet the men, I'd probably form a bond with them. Previously, I'd walled myself off from that possibility, but my interview with Professor M. piqued my curiosity.

Prior to the visit, prison officials told me I had ninety minutes to interview five men. I came prepared with two simple questions: *Who were you when you came here? & Who are you now?* Because no recording devices or cameras were allowed, I took notes on everything I experienced, hoping to capture the look and feel of the prison. Hastily scribbled sentences contained every detail I observed—the yellow X on the elevator floor designating the spot where no one could stand for fear of stalling the elevator, the insulation peeling off of the pipes, the black metal peeking through chipped paint on the bars, the smell of bleach in the hallway outside the school, the song-like Baltimore and foreign dialects of the guards.

Professor M. had told the men why I was coming, and then gave them a bit of my background—college lecturer, writer, and former high school teacher. After about fifteen minutes of introductions and chatting, we got started with the business of the interviews. Each man sat around a large, rectangular table with a black and white composition book that held his writing. I didn't think we'd have time for sharing, but it was good to see that they'd come prepared. I made notes about the physical condition of the room and copied down the quote written in neat cursive on wide yellow bulletin-board paper that served as the backdrop on the stage. "Education is a passport to the future, for tomorrow belongs to those who prepare for it."

The men laughed and joked with one another and shared stories with Professor M. and me. I felt much more relaxed than I'd imagined, and I was totally enthralled with all that the men had to share about their lives. Here is a sample of what they told me. All of the men's names have been changed to preserve their anonymity.

> I was misguided. I had no sense of self-worth. I grew up without any guidance. I'd say I was a lost individual. I was only reading at about the 7th-grade level. I did some dumb things. I've been here since I was 15 and now I'm 28…"
> ~ Ryan, from East Baltimore

> The first time I was in prison, there were no programs and no education classes. But now, I take every program they offer here. I know how to make sense of my life. That took maturation. What I want to do now is put a new vibe into the system—something that will be beneficial for myself and others.
> ~ Matt, from East Baltimore

> When I came here, I had just turned 15. I grew up in the child-care system, so I lived in lots of places. Coming to prison was like crossing the Rubicon for me. Since I've been here, I've developed my values and formed better habits. I love reading—one of my favorite authors is Proust… I'd describe myself as a lover of language, and I live in my imagination. I've developed a value set and for me, the most important value is compassion. I see myself as part of the human family. I know that spirituality is omnipresent, and it connects all of us through one language—the language of love.
> ~Vincent, grew up in various MD and DC foster care homes and institutions

I had never expected to hear the kinds of stories they were telling me, and I was amazed at how open and trusting they were of a complete stranger. Professor M. and I said a hasty farewell when the guards came in to tell the men they had to return to the tiers—the cells where they lived. Each man shook my hand and asked me to return. Matt's last words to us before the group broke up touched me deeply and remained with me to inspire my return visit: "When people are in a state of disconnection, it's much easier to harm the environment, to harm each other. The arts build a connection. That's why they're so important." I felt the same way about the arts and knew I had something to contribute to these men who were all so eager to learn and make new lives for themselves.

When I began working as an official volunteer, I coped with the juxtaposition of sadness and despair of both the prison environment and the men's stories by taking copious notes. There were times when it felt like the men were speaking in poetry, their observations where so keen and nuanced. And writing poetry about my experiences was the best way for me to process my sadness and frequent rage at the injustices I witnessed. In *Nine Gates: Entering the Mind of Poetry*, poet Jane Hirschfield expands on poetry's ability to capture intense feelings when she observes that, "Through poetry's concentration, great sweeps of thought, emotion, and perception are compressed to forms the mind is able to hold—into images, sentences, and stories that serve as entrance tokens to large and often slippery realms of being."

Poetry offers the perfect tool for capturing the essence of an experience. And because I was usually torn between giving the men my full attention and taking notes about what they were saying, poetry suited the way that I collected impressions in snippets of conversation and brief phrases of description. With our time limited to 90 minutes and a rigidly-enforced schedule, an air of urgency pervaded our meetings. Professor M. and I needed time for a check-in to hear how the men were doing, and we reserved time for each member of the group to read something they had written either as a draft or in a more polished form. But because we were in a prison, we also felt a responsibility to respond to any unexpected events that might come up—a lockdown that had gone on for days, a friend being placed in solitary for several weeks, the loss of recreation time. When the men talked about their daily lives and difficulties, I felt compelled to record some of the details of their discussion. An event like spending time in solitary for circulating a petition for better food became more than a news item on the radio—and I wanted to capture the details so that I could share the truth of the men's experiences.

Reporters frequently say that the United States incarcerates more people than any other nation in the world, but what does that reality look like?

According to a 2018 report from The Prison Policy Initiative called "Mass Incarceration: The Whole Pie," authors Wagner and Sawyer detail the numbers of America's incarcerated people in numerous types of confinement. According to one of Prison Policy's factsheets, "The American criminal justice system holds almost 2.3 million people in 1,719 state prisons, 102 federal prisons, 1,852 juvenile facilities, 3,163 local jails, and 80 Indian Country jails as well as military prisons, immigration detention facilities, civil commitment centers, state psychiatric hospitals, and prisons in U.S. territories." Yet despite the massive scope of the U. S. prison population, very few people have ever been inside a prison and fewer still have talked with incarcerated people to find out who they are underneath the label of felon.

Before I volunteered in a prison, I was one of those people, and I had no idea who the prisoners were, as men and women with lives and families, until I ventured inside. What I found was so compelling that I wanted to share the experience and the lives of the folks inside with an audience. And while statistics and data do tell a large part of the story, I knew that poetry could capture voices and experiences in a visceral way that might move people to want to learn more about the ways prisons work and to develop some empathy for the millions of people in the United States who live and work behind bars.

ARTIST'S STATEMENT

At the age of 46, I stood my ground against a violent sociopath who had abused and tortured me. In doing so, I preserved my own life and the lives of my children. But as a result of that choice to protect me and my family, I spent the next 13 years incarcerated in a Utah state prison. My lifelong career in art of sculpting through mixed medium was suddenly reduced to working only with scrap paper, a Bic pen, and a handful of colored pencils. Three years in, I mastered the art of crochet and resumed sculpting for a variety of venues, including the Hogle Zoo in Utah; Muckenthaler Museum in California; Dialog Through Translation in Helsinki; President Lincoln's Cottage Museum in Washington, DC; Justice Arts Coalition; and State of Utah Museums.

    This drawing, entitled "You Will Not Waste My Life," represents the transition from institutional victim to defiant survivor. Even though the state had essentially picked up where my abusive spouse had left off, through my art, I gave voice to my experiences. Art gave me the will to survive, communicate, educate, and encourage others to do the same.

FENCE

Fence   a defense
a protection   a barrier
It makes for a good neighbor
or the name of an August Wilson play.

Fence   a boundary or a means of protection
as in the city erects fences to prevent
homeless people from camping under bridges.

The verb   to fence   means to avoid giving a direct reply
to be evasive or to parry as when federal officials
bob and weave with reporters scrambling to uncover the truth
about the forgotten ones in Guantanamo   or Attica   or Cumberland.

Those same officials call solitary for 23 hours a day
administrative segregation   or refer to forced tube-feeding
as saving a hunger-striker's life. Or call waterboarding
enhanced interrogation.

Every day we find ourselves engaged
in removing barriers, dismantling verbal parries.
Eager to begin fence-mending.

THE CODE

In this circle of men,
their code demands one rule—
find my worth in my words.

Each session, a blank check
you discover that everyone has
an attic filled with hope,
loss, and longing.

How do you hold the experience
of terse words
shaped by
poverty and despair?

Slowly, you discover the unexpected bridges
connecting your life to theirs—the falls,
the disappointing parents,
the harsh, invisible walls of privilege.

Press deeper,
mind only the present.
The books discussed,
the ideas on the page.

PASSAGE TO POSSIBILITY

Black and white and shades of gray
capture everything I see.
Sometimes, a flash of color tricks the eye—a lone orange jumpsuit,

the trampled fibers of the red carpet
in the elevator,
the pink of an ID badge.

Today I discover the tunnel that connects the education building to the tiers.
The classroom wing is locked, or maybe the lock is broken.
The familiar red door doesn't yield an entry when I ring the buzzer.

The guards behind the locked door
wave to me at the end of the hallway
and point me to an unfamiliar entrance.

I shrug my shoulders and shake my head,
afraid to walk in places I don't know.
A man from the writing group beckons me to follow.

I walk through another set of barred doors—thick black iron-barred doors,
a black guard in a black uniform waves me through.
I find myself in a tunnel

as wide as a city street—high roof, drab walls.
Imprisoned men wearing gray DOC garb or white kitchen uniforms
fill the tunnel. And I realize—all these men could be on the outside

maybe working as a shopkeeper, or a minister,
maybe walking kids home from school, or playing ball in the park.

But today they stream through this vast underground tunnel—
back and forth
caught between now and possibility.

TRANSMUTE

To change from one form, species, condition, or nature to another.
—*Webster's Collegiate Dictionary*
You have to go back for the snakes if you really want to heal.
—heard on Fresh Air interview

Arms weighted with snakes

writhing, cold, slimy

scales flash, tongues dart. Snakes

sanctuaried under ancient rocks

shame & torment buried in vain.

Imagine you can

transmute the original struggle,

the spiral of loss,

the slam of betrayal.

Shed the skin

of refusal.

LOCK ME UP

out here in Elsewhere
& I won't ask you
to reconsider how living
90 miles away from home
            burdens my family by design.
Respect the rules
a mantra the guards repeat as
I'm strip-searched after each visit.
Respect isn't a duality
in my world
           where a tossed dish
                    lands me in the hole
a cauldron of despair.

The fire of one more submission
seers my heart with a fresh rage
                   yet I have no place to scream.
I am slowly learning
that no exposure of who I am
OR
who I am becoming
can erase the dark contours of my past.

WHAT I THINK ABOUT
—in the voice of an imprisoned man

My deepest fear is that no one waits for me.
I sit in a barred cell, live next to a steel toilet, stained and reeking.
"You're nothing but an animal," the guard tells me, as he opens my cage twice a day.

Daily, I forgive myself, my younger self,
so angry, so charged
and reckless.

My younger self—no tools but swagger and steel stuffed under a mattress.
I wish I could tell that boy how his grandma and baby sister loved him—
but he pushed away all that kind of talk.

"I don't need y'all," he'd say.
"Don't need nothing from nobody."
I hear those words bounce off the walls and fill my cell with their echoes.
I weep for forgiveness.

SHE LITERALLY WORKED HERSELF TO DEATH

I'm curious about her dedication
about the way she pressed
her black uniform
before she left
for the 3pm shift at the prison.
She literally
        worked herself to death.

25 years of faithful service—
no sick days, no extra time off.
She worked double shifts
because the prison couldn't hire enough qualified folks
to replace the older ones
who were bone-tired
or achy with stress.
She literally
        worked herself to death.

When she missed a shift,
a friend went to her house
        found her   dead
sitting upright on the couch, dressed in her black uniform,
clear plastic lunch box packed with dinner.
The chaplain claims
she literally
        worked herself to death.

SURVIVING THE LAKE IN THE BASEMENT

If these brick walls could speak, what stories would they tell?
Would people point and shout "Liar" at the tales, impossible to fathom?
As we descend into the bowels of the prison

I shudder and hesitate—it sounds like a fight brewing.
Instead we see men in gray prison garb wielding wet vacs and wringing out sodden towels.
Brown water fills an endless row of buckets.

The lake in the hallway is finally being drained, after
water-logged, gray mop-heads walled it off for over two months.
Fetid water that pooled and grew
courtesy of a leaky pipe behind a crumbling cinderblock wall.

Weeks before, an employee confided, "Officials tell us it will cost $100,000 to fix the leak."
When I talk to him about slipping or the dangers of what grows in the water, he tells me
"It's easier to work here if you pretend not to see things."

But now, my friend and I smile as we step around the shrinking puddles
on our way into the school.
The men in the cleaning crew nod in recognition,
happy to be of use.

Two hours later when my friend and I leave the school,
after working with the only man who showed up for our writing group,
the lake has reappeared.

Outside, murky water pools in the low-end of the blacktop driveway.
Two geese paddle slowly past us, dunk their heads, and
shower us with water
as they shake their feathers clean.

$1 AN HOUR TO FIGHT LARGEST FIRE IN CALIFORNIA
　　—based on a story from *Democracy Now*, August, 2018

Because I'm a prisoner, I put my life on the line
for $2.00 a day + $1.00 an hour when I'm fighting fires.
I've protected California
I saved thousands of dollars' worth of property—

I've got training in wildland firefighting.
And I'd love to be a firefighter when I get out.
But I need a few fire science credits & some college credits.
The biggest problem staring me down?
I can't get licensed as an EMT
because I have a record.

What kind of sense does that make?
—if all my training and experience
is enough to fight fires while I'm incarcerated,
it should be enough to fight fires once I'm free.

You know how I could live if I was a real firefighter?
I could give my children a sweet little house
Maybe even send them to college—if I made the $74,000 a year
like a regular firefighter.

When I first got here
I worked in the office, but after a while,
I knew too much
so they moved me outside to work landscaping.
But I'm real allergic to poison oak.
So, if I breathe in that stuff,
my throat can close up & I could die.
I figured I might as well be on the fire line if that was the case.

I didn't *volunteer* to go to prison.
I didn't *volunteer* to go to fire camp
and fight fires.
I want to go back to my family
and my children.

Note: In September of 2020, the California governor signed a bill that would allow inmate firefighters to have their records expunged, clearing the way for them to become certified as Emergency Medical Technicians, a requirement to become a firefighter.

INFORMATION BULLETIN: BOOK ORDERS

"Inmates shall be allowed quarterly
book orders from 3 companies.
No third-party orders are allowed."

The first approved seller is Penguin Books.
I place a mock-order for several titles. The "buy" button drops down a list of sellers
Amazon, Barnes & Noble, Books-a-Million, Target and Walmart.
Millions of books sold on Amazon come from 3rd party sellers.

Books & Things from Utah is the second approved vender
& I notice the top-seller on the home page
   The Book of Mormon Made Easier
How many Mormons are in Maryland prisons?

The last approved company—Edward R. Hamilton Books
has 16 selections under the heading "African American"
including *The Boleyn Women*.
 I thought they were British aristocracy—not African American.
Prices range from $4.95 to $19.95 per book. All shipping is $4.00 per order.

"Inmates shall submit their orders to the property officer for review.
Inmates are allowed a maximum capacity of 1.5 cubic feet of books
12" X 12" x 18".
Therefore, inmates may not possess more than ten books.
To meet these requirements
inmates may need to mail out books
or donate books to the prison library
upon receipt of new books."

The men tell me
there are no limits on TVs or Game Boys in the cells.

SANDBAGS AGAINST THE FLOOD

When the writing teacher asks
"Where's Marco?"

Daryl tells her, *He's in C. L. A. P.*
Character Literacy Awareness Project

A class where the old guys teach the young ones
what it means to be a man.

When a writing teacher
asks the men

"What do you need to prepare you
for life outside…besides a GED?"

The answers pour out
like a Greek chorus—

It's overwhelming to leave here—
I came in when I was 16.

How do I rent an apartment?
Housing, driver's license, job—

I don't know where to start
The men's needs stacking

like sandbags against a flood.
Daryl adds one more thought

before he returns to the tiers—
We don't know how to be citizens.

PAINT CHIPS OF MEMORY: BALTIMORE BURNING 1968 AND 2015

Rust
pits the borders of the old Reads Drugstore sign
gaunt as a man's cheeks hollow from hunger.
No one strolls the aisles leafing through magazines,
No one sits on the chrome lunch-counter stools.
A national landmark on a once grand street now bears witness
to homeless veterans and nodding runaways.

Pilgrimage foliage
The color of the brick walls surrounding my high school
as National Guard troops patrol Gay Street.
Pilgrimage foliage
the color of the brick homes we called projects
a chain-linked fence surrounding the dirt yard
where girls jump rope and boys ride raggedy bikes.

Aztec Brick
The CVS neon sign blinking in the night,
the color of the flames licking the squad cars
the night charged with the dynamic blue energy
of police dressed in storm-trooper armor.
"We gave them space to destroy," the mayor says,
and stands unapologetic when asked to recant.
I watch at home on television
to see history repeating itself
like a Greek Chorus in endless lament.

A VISIT TO CONSTITUTION STREET

Sunday morning. Baltimore City. A car speeds past me.

GPS guides me to Central Booking and Intake Center

My first visit to a friend. The only friend I know who's ever been to prison.

Some call him a martyr on the altar of ambition for our city's state's attorney.

Many believe he's innocent, but he can't get bail.
Two months in Baltimore Central Booking.
So crowded he sleeps on the floor in the gym. Showers once every week or so.

"I take care of my hygiene with a cat bath," he wrote in a letter.

Fallsway to Madison to Constitution Street.

Where the city hides all of its jails. Constitution Street, absent from all traffic reports

as in, "There's a backup on Constitution Street. All police should use another route if

traveling to Central Booking this afternoon. Now back to you, Stan."

Constitution Street—lined with prisons.

Brick fortresses from the turn of the 20th century. Tan concrete buildings from the 60s.

Each one festooned with razor wire, gleaming in the April sunlight.

Ring the buzzer to enter. Finger prints on a screen. Pro forma pat-down.

The guard doesn't look for drugs on the bottoms of my feet.

She speaks kindly to everyone.

Ride the elevator with mothers, fathers, babies in strollers.

We are buzzed into the glass waiting area, then buzzed into the hallway

that functions like a chute for visitors spitting them into glass-walled cages.

Each cubicle holds two people on the free side and one man on the inside.

My friend smiles as I enter the cage to talk with him. He puts his hand on the glass.

I match my palm to his. Tears well in his eyes. We pray together.

His sturdy hand wipes his cheeks clean. "I've never seen you in a jumpsuit," I tell him.

"Yellow is not your color."

DRESS CODE FOR THE WOMEN'S PRISON

They won't let you in. My friend insists.
The assistant warden makes up her own rules.
Don't think you can go braless either.
Wear a sports bra.

No jeans.
No leggings.
No sheer blouses.
No halters.
No mini-skirts.
No open-toed shoes.

The list by the door must have had 20 prohibitions.
Most make sense. My friend adds one more:

No underwire bras.

"That's the only kind I wear," I tell her.
"It's stupid to buy a new bra to volunteer in the women's prison.
"I wear underwires in the men's prison all the time—
The alarm never goes off."

I imagine the scenario. I arrive as a new volunteer.
in a place where a pen can be turned into a weapon.
Someone deduces that I'm wearing an underwire bra.
Then what? How does an imprisoned woman
corner me so that the guards don't notice?

I imagine the scenario—would she
slit open the fabric and remove the underwires?
Does she risk taking both?
I imagine the scenario—
maybe we slip into an unmonitored toilet stall,
switch bras, and she wears
the hidden weapons back onto her tier.

ELEVATOR RULES

Wait for the barred gates to slide open.
Stand in the cramped space
between the open hallway and the elevator door.
There's no escape,
but you're used to feeling trapped by now.

Used to the grimy red carpet on the floor,
the pungent mix of perfume and after-shave,
the cadence of Caribbean and Baltimore accents.

You know to look for a free space
when the elevator is nearly full.
You make sure that no one is standing
in the yellow, taped-off square
with an "X" in the middle.

You hear your friend's warning every
time you ride in the box—"Don't stand on the yellow X.
The elevator will get stuck."
Everyone knows that rule. Everyone obeys.

But what do you do
when the elevator door opens
and you see three men—
one guard pressed up against the wall, a prisoner facing you,
his hands bound with heavy, steel chains,
and a guard next to him
holding more chains.

The three of you look at each other.
One second, two.
"Where are you going?" the guard asks.
To the basement, you answer,
and step inside.

IN NEED OF A PHONE

After the elevator door slides open
after the guard unlocks the barred gate
a sign on the wall catches your eye.
You silently mouth the letters
P.R.E.A.
to yourself, then click
through your memories for an answer.

Now keep walking down the hallways
don't gamble on anyone explaining the acronym
P.R.E.A.
Carry yourself confidently, edging your way
deeper into the tunnels of the prison, where the
classrooms are buried in the basement.
Every six feet or so, a
P.R.E.A.
sign stenciled on the wall.

Spanish and English words direct
anyone who knows of a violation
to report the incident to an 800 number.

Suddenly you flash back
to orientation, remember the warning—
Prison Rape Elimination Act—a new law.

I'M NOT LOOKING FOR MERCY
~a found poem based on a YouTube video of a death-row inmate

I have a moral code and a clear conscience. No women, no children,
no innocent people have suffered at my hands. The guy I murdered—
he was a meth dealer—guilty as hell. I've always lived
outside the law. In high school I sold pot and LSD.
Got married and had a son,
then decided to be a male stripper and run a landscaping gig in the daytime.
Know this: when you live beyond the law, sometimes
you react way harsher than people on the outside can figure. You got to,
or people think you're soft.

So, I'm not asking for mercy.

You know what they call people like me?
They call us volunteers. I dropped my appeals back in 2006
and told the state of Nevada to put me in the execution line.
'Cause in here—this is no life. I can't go outside.
I can't walk more than five steps in any direction. The only relationships I have
are behind glass and across a table in the visiting room.

Killing that guy was wrong, and I'll take what's coming.
But now the word is the execution is postponed.
The state can't get the drugs they need because no company wants to be known
as a death dealer. I'm not afraid of much,
but I'd rather face a firing squad than take the drug cocktail I've heard about.
Midazolam—a painkiller, cisatracurium—a paralytic,
and fentanyl—an opioid. That crap kills people left and right.
I've been reading up on executions, and some states allow death
by electrocution, or lethal gas, or hanging.
Me?
I'll face the firing squad
before they shoot me up with fentanyl.

WALKING BY THE SCHOOL YARD

    —in response to Betsy DeVos's Senate confirmation

Neglect is a sin of omission
Deny
rag-
bound
books
Deny
children's
dreams
abandoned
Deny
Omission is a sin of neglect.

On Driving by a City School

Hope abandoned
Broken
water-fountains
heaters
windows
Broken
hearts
communities
spirits
Broken
Abandoned hope.

On Driving by a Prison Complex

Easy to ignore those people.
Lost
education
rights
meaning
Lost
souls
crushed
forsaken
Lost
Those people—easy to ignore.

FLOWERS IN PRISON

Barbed wire stacked
four feet high
stuffs the spaces
in between
triple rows of fencing.

Water on the path
pools at the curb
dry patches form
informal crosswalk
straddling single lanes
of the walkway.

She steps around
soft piles of green
goose droppings,
notes the stains
on the concrete.

Loose black soil
frames each side
of the path.
Stuck in the dirt
like lonely children
marigolds—every four inches.

Who planted them?
Who waters them?
She notes the brown tinges of
decay on the fringed leaves.
Flowers
struggling towards the light.

LODESTARS IN THE BASEMENT

Today four men gather in the prison basement
for the writing group
all foolish enough
to conjure hope despite
the rusty chairs, duct-taped pipes,
and being counted by three different officers
in under 90 minutes.

Rule #1 Beware of passing notes

Leonard passes me a note,
the paper short and narrow
like a receipt.
"Three things I want to learn:
grammar
vocabulary
poetry
I also want to learn history
but I don't know where to start."

Rule #2: Beware of prisoner's requests

"Please teach me more
about poetry," CR says.
"Tell me about iambic pentameter."
I start with the 10 syllables and demonstrate
stressed and unstressed—
the men shrug until
Gus stands and performs his poem.
He pounds out the rhythm of his lines
with his fist against his chest:
"How do I grow on a farm
with a surface made of bricks?"

Rule #3: Beware of model behavior

Marco stands to read,
his dark hair close-cropped.
Tattoos cover his arms and his neck,
markers of his life before.
But as he reads, his voice strong and clear, his face shining—

I glimpse the boy he used to be,
before the sorrow, before the foolish choices.
"I'm trying to find myself
but my cell-mate
he doesn't do anything but lie on his bunk.
I tell him—read, write, do something, man.
I share my books with him.
Then I think he might be
blocking himself."

MAINTENANCE

In a place
where water
can be a curse
puddles in the corner
reek of chemicals
and etch the tiles
brown with stains.

Plastic buckets
in the hallway
brim with
gray water—
bugs float atop
rafts of
sodden drywall.

Trays rigged
to the ceiling
with steel straps
catch the steady
trickle of water.

For over two months
a leaking pipe
creates a lake in the hallway.
Cotton mop-heads
contain the fetid water.

When I point out the dangers—mold, slipping, bugs—
one of the counselors tells me
"Those of us who work here
have learned to walk around it."

MY SISTER BROUGHT ME A GIFT (JC SPEAKS ABOUT HIS WORK)

I wrote this book about ten years ago and
sent it out all over the place, looking for a publisher.
When no one took it,
I stopped writing.
Then my twin sister came to visit me a few weeks ago—
she handed me this binder full of my poems and said,
"Here's a gift for you. Are you still writing?"

One thought came back to me as I read
my poem called "A Plea for Love."
I dedicated my book to all the poets
whose work has inspired me—
Maya Angelou, Ralph Waldo Emerson,
Paul Laurence Dunbar, Langston Hughes,
William Shakespeare.
They fill my heart.

As I read my old work,
I remembered what I love about writing.
When I had a cell all to myself,
I posted sticky notes all over the walls
with ideas for characters in a novel.
Each one had dialogue—those notes covered my cell.
I was so immersed in the world of my book—
I wanted to live there.

Poetry is my relationship to everything that's alive—
it motivates me.
When I read someone else's work, it touches my heart.
I am joined to them by our mutual feelings.
My hope is that when I write,
someone can then use my words as a
tool for motivation.

LETTER FROM A BALTIMORE JAIL
   —a found poem

I face these four enemy walls—this cell
robbing me of my desire to live.
The courts have no care
for my real story—to let them tell it
no Black man with a prior criminal history
would drive
away from gunshots.

I've been writing a lot lately—the most important part of me.
My true freedom within these pages.
I've written to my girlfriend every day, 20 new poems, and the start of a new book called
My Second Chance.

I'm in the cell 23 hours a day
since January 29th.
Today is Valentine's and I finally get a shower.
I've maintained my hygiene with a bird-bath at the sink.

At first, I had no pen, no paper—
there's no library here.
I read the Bible every day and take beautiful lessons from it.
There's so much riding on my case.

I want to *prove* that men can change
or else
others will fall victim
to this wicked system.

When I get more paper
I'll copy my poems for you.
I'm down to 10 pieces—using every one strategically.
I send you all of my love.

NATHANIEL BREAKS IT DOWN FOR ME

Dreadlocks hang to his waist
his lean form erect
as he shakes my hand.
Gray work-shirt, gray pants
Nathaniel always carries a book—
One day it's *The History of Africa*
as thick as the Oxford Dictionary.
One day it's *The Mis-Education of the American Negro*—
a slim volume he tucks into his writing folder.

His voice—deep and mellow,
his dark eyes search my face
as if unravelling a mystery.

"Do you work?" I ask,
not knowing where to begin.
Nathaniel leans forward
                        folds his hands on the table.
I'm still considered too dangerous to have a job.
He shakes his head and moves his book aside.
I used to be in a gang. I'm not anymore,
                        but it doesn't matter.

GED but no more education—
He talks of childhood—
I remember when I was 8 years old
going to my grandmother's house after school—
reading stories—she always had time for me.

NO SUGAR INSIDE

The yoke of rules
and counts
firmly in place
a collar around their necks—
when to answer,
when to be silent.

Imprisoned men
understand
divide and conquer
arbitrary routines
waiting in line
until each man
enters his cell
at the same time.

The men grumble
shake their heads—
*They won't let us
make taffy anymore.*
a rigged recipe
of drink mix,
coffee creamer,
and water.

The Corrections Officers say
"You're cooking drugs
in there."
Guys just want
a taste of sweetness.
But today
the microwaves
are silent.

PARKING LOT RENDEZVOUS

A chance encounter with a friend—both of you
in the same location—you need to talk.

But you're not meeting at the country club
in a posh suburb, hoping to see someone after a swim.

You're arranging to meet
with the prison's chaplain.

The first time he told you "Maybe I'll see you at 2 pm on the parking lot"
was amusing. The second time signals a strong message

Communication is monitored, we're all watched.
Those guards behind the walls, on the parking lot —so nice to your face

bored in their towers—see you step out of your car,
scan the parking lot

for the white robe and simple taqiyah of the chaplain.
You walk towards each other—guileless

in your mission
to deliver a brown envelope of short stories for the men.

Taqiyah: a rounded skullcap worn by Muslim men to cover their heads at prayer-time and during the day

PRIVILEGE

Orient yourself to the scene
one man speaking to another
separated by a vacuum of power
a trespass of privilege.

The imprisoned man places his documents on the table,
harnesses his courage.
Maybe this time he's got enough certificates—
barber school, alternatives to violence, kitchen management.

Fluent in the language of subservience
he answers the parole officer's questions,
"Yes, sir. Thank you, sir."
Maybe this time—a respite for his accomplishments.

Congratulations, you've done a lot since I last saw you.
The parole officer thumbs through the file and then
pushes it back across the table.
Come back in two years.

REAL FOR REAL
—in a prisoner's writing group

Keepin' it real~ real deal~raw story

Doesn't happen all at once

broken home, broken mind, broken laws

TURNing pages, turning AWAY, turning off

count time~count me~no-count Mitch

locked down   for standing up

CONflict resolution?   denied PETITIONS

He stands up, they ship him out

food complaints~wilted lettuce~peppered with grit & dirt

rat FECES on unwashed TRAYS

"Who asked for that book?"   "…it's for my dAUGHTer"

Velveteen Rabbit wants TO BE REAL

"When you're real, you don't MIND being HURT."

boy and bunny   "I'm starting to feel sad." the men relate

age doesn't matter~message connects~wanting love

"The Lion King…taught us too." about jealousy and the MEANing of Betrayal.

becoming REAL. "WE'RE REAL" for REAL

JC SITS IN SOLITARY

They tell me that Beauty lives everywhere
but I've never seen it.
They tell me that Beauty contains
alchemical properties
capable of transforming a man's fortune,
but I don't see Beauty
walking through this concrete abyss—
No different from my old street with
boarded up, vacant houses,
my old school with broken windows and metal detectors.
Beauty would turn away from the routine of
gray slop on metal trays—meals
shoved through a tiny portal twice a day.
Some days I remember how my parents raised me
with Halleluiah and go to school,
while my minister charged me to love Jesus
and throttle Satan.
Now I sit with this loss—
my only task—survival.
The promise of Beauty
another mirage on the mildewed concrete wall.

RICHARD STURN'S RULES FOR PARTICIPATION

Richard's tan pants hang straight from his waist
full and loose, stop inches above his ankles.
White socks turned down top off brown boots.
His hair is cropped close, black framed glasses

shield his dark eyes.
His coarse beard runs
           from ear to ear, like thick fringe
                        starched and dry.

He comes to every session, never shares.
I start with *How are you? What have you been reading?*
Richard says, "I don't have time to read.
Too busy working on stuff for my release."

When the other men ask *What have you got today?*
We see you writing all the time in that book.
Richard tells the writing group
                "I got some work. But I ain't sharing it.
                        I don't share with nobody."

He defends the one teacher
everyone else fears—and finds aloof.
"She helped me. She's just trying to do her job.
Tighten things up around here."

The men look down at the table.
We sense the invisible wall
           he builds with each phrase.
                Richard folds his arms across his chest—the other men read.

Then he tells us, "I'm leaving soon—
going to a half-way house."
Will you have a job? I ask and pull back in my chair.
An offer of space.

"I'm going to do haz mat.
Been doing that here in the prison."
               Then Richard leaves the group, clutching his Quaran
                      to pray in an empty room.

SAVED BY KINDNESS

Rain pounds on the roof—
you jump when the roar
of thunder rolls
through the floors
like a sonic wave.

No umbrella.
No raincoat.
The deluge
creates a river in the path you must cross.

A man standing by the door
wearing a green polo shirt
offers you a plastic bag.

"Hold your books and your purse
close to your body," he tells you
then slips the long plastic bag
over your shoulders
until your head
pops through
the hole torn in the top.

You walk out
into the storm
wrapped in the clear
mantle of kindness.

SAYING GOODBYE

Christopher returned to the writing group
after being absent for several weeks.
He writes fiction, so I gave him
an *Anthology of the Best American Short Stories*.

Weeks later he sits across from me in the circle,
his solemn eyes on his notebook, but as I ask what he's
been reading, he sits up straighter.
Remember that anthology you gave me?
I've read 700 pages.

Christopher's been in prison since he was 16 years old.
Last week he turned 40.
When he reads his latest short story, I hear the power in
his prose—the way he weaves a tapestry
with strands of character, dialog, and setting.

Later, the conversation drifts to the guys who have left—never saying good-bye.
I watch the men's faces as they nod automatically in agreement. Then I tell them,
"It's hard when people leave without a word. Especially after sharing so much in
the group. Closure is important."

Christopher speaks to me in the hallway,
after the other men have drifted back to the tiers.
I hold my notebook to my chest and lean against the dented door.
He focuses on my face and says, *I've been working with a lawyer,*
getting my sentence reduced, so I have a lot to clear up.
That's why I haven't been to the group.

I thank him for telling me and wish him well.
Christopher looks down at the ground, then says,
It's not my fault that I didn't know about saying good-bye.
I was raised in a prison.

THE LITERARY DAY OF THE ARTS

The prison library hums and pulses
with musicians practicing original tunes.
The tattooed emcee performs a final mic check.

A few guards are scattered in the crowd,
along with the Muslim chaplain and two social workers
sitting in the audience.

As I settle into my seat, I remember
what one of the guards cautioned
as I went through screening:

"We had a lockdown earlier,
but things are OK now."
He shrugged. I nodded.

As I wait for the performances to begin
a chill of fear paralyzes my body.
What am I doing in the basement of a men's prison?

Images of hostage-taking men
flash into my mind. In another flash, I return to the library
when Anderson, the star of the writing group,

steps to the front of the room.
"Welcome, everyone, to our second
annual literary day of the arts."

One by one he calls up his colleagues from the group,
and I hear their words in a new way—accompanied by images on the screen,
personal artwork, music from their friends.

A hush of respect falls over the room.
At the end of the reading, someone lets
me know that it's Anderson's birthday.

In the back of the room, men line up
for cartons of orange drink and single cookies wrapped in plastic.
One of each per person.

I wish I could have brought you a cake, Anderson, but I'm not allowed.
He smiles at me and nods.
"That's OK, Ms. B. This is as good as it gets for a birthday in the joint."

THE MENTAL HEALTH BOX

It must be purposeful—the green container affixed to the wall.
The lid flush against the box, bound with a lock.
Doesn't take up much space.

I feel foolish when I tell the social worker—
"Every week when I walk by, I wonder what's in
the mental health box."

I imagine torn pieces of paper—
men filling the box with
furtively written requests, stuffed in as they walk past.

Please don't restrict my visitors.
My cell-mate has been in solitary for a year. When's he getting out?
Why can't we have college classes? I need a fan in my cell, please.

The social worker is silent,
then she shakes her head.
"I have no idea what's in that box."

HOPE ON HOLD

Once you're inside
ignore the wreckage
of time, the lined faces
of men gray with age,
the once-cagey 16-year-old,
the disorganized shuffle
of papers, of rules, of feet.
The torpor of boredom
thick as dreams
of honey on toast.
Once you're inside
every smile is suspect,
every glance a risk.
Even hope tucks into a corner
when these doors groan closed.

THE WOMEN'S PRISON

After a cursory pat-down, the female officer flips through my papers.
The therapist meets me after screening,
then she leads me outside and across a wide compound

littered with great piles of fresh goose guano.
Who can live here?
The red brick buildings scarred with age,

the double and triple
coils of razor wire surrounding the compound.
Who could imagine such a climb to be free?

The utter lack of beauty—
is it meant to kill desire?
I go with my promises clear—to return just once more.

They'll work on you, the therapist cautions. *You'll want to come back.*
She pushes a button and the guard buzzes us into a one-story brick structure.
I hear voices in a distant room,

and the clang of the doors locking behind me.
We enter the space where I'll hold the writing class
then drag the dust-covered table to the center of the room.

The therapist disappears to gather the women
while I unstack plastic chairs and place them around the table.
I notice paint peeling off iron bars on the windows,

piles of dirt on the floor, the whiteboard with "father" and "abandoned"
scrawled in fading marker.
Five women file in wearing baggy burgundy cotton tops and pants—

one has a sparkling of jewelry, one is heavily tattooed.
They greet me with shy smiles and expectant notebooks.
"You're the first new person who's come here in seven years."

After we write for a while, they tell me
"The men have more opportunities than we do,
but we have TVs in our cells."

"You know what makes a difference here?"
"People let us know that we have gifts."
"We never knew we could be anything special."

VISITING ROOM

Across from the visiting room
filled with comfortable chairs,
a few sofas, and a table or two—
visitors and imprisoned women
gaze at a wordless warning across the hall.

The corrections officer sits behind
a glass wall and supervises the sign-in process.
Behind her—a frame about 6 feet across
and 5 feet high with 3 rows of handcuffs
carefully arranged by size,
a number visible inside the circle of each cuff.

The first few cuffs—small enough for a young girl
of 8 or 9, graduating to cuffs that could easily
fit the wrists or ankles of a large woman.
Beneath the cuffs are rows of chains—any combination
of cuffs and chains is possible—each chain longer,
each link heavier and thicker. The cuffs and chains
cold, silent reminders
lining the shadow box across the hall.

WHERE'S MITCH?

"He's in solitary—been there for two weeks,"
the men tell me.

Locked up for 23 hours a day.
What did he do?

"You know Mitch," the men all chorus.
"He knows his rights, so he don't take no crap."

Mitch wrote letters, to all kinds of people.
"They don't like that."

I remember the furtive moments in the hallway
talking with Mitch after the writing group dispersed.

Mitch told me about his wages for working in the prison factory
"I get paid really well—$80 a month for painting state logos on cars and buses."

"The kitchen guys—they make about $40, but the guys who clean
the floors and bathrooms, they only make about $20."

And one day Mitch told me that the state visitors had come
"My boss said I could speak to them about concerns.

"I told them about the reprisals," he said, "for when we complain—
and later my boss told me to shut up."

Then there was the committee collecting testimony on solitary confinement.
In the hallway, always in the hallway after the writing group, Mitch said,

"There's an old guy here, he was locked up in solitary for seven years.
When I asked him to write a letter about it, he could only write three sentences."

That's torture, I blurt. *The UN says any more than 15 days.*
"I was locked up for four years," Mitch confided.

So, what was he complaining about? I asked the men.
"Rat feces in the food. Now he's in the hole."

WHAT THEY NEED

I move through the sea of men in gray
as they gather in the library for the show.
Posters on the wall encourage reading, working hard.

One man approaches me and offers his hand.
I'm getting out in a few weeks, he tells me. *I really need a job.*
"What have they taught you in the prison?" I ask.

He shrugs his shoulders. *All we have here is GED classes
and I finished them a long time ago.*
Our eyes search each other's faces.

"I'll pray for you," is all I can give.
When I ask another man what would have made school meaningful,
he nearly charges at me, raises his hands over his head,

moving them in time with his words.
*Nonviolent conflict resolution. They're teaching us now,
but we needed it a long time ago.*

SESSIONS WITH RODRIGO

I: Rodrigo

I've turned my cell into a classroom—You know, it's either Yale or jail. I write all day. That TV, it calls to me, those games just waiting, but I got books in me. I'm doing 30 years. I got my GED, yes, in prison. But school never meant nothing to me. Math? Math never taught me about H-U-N-G-E-R. I knew that first-hand when I went home. I did read a book once, but that's about all I ever got outta school. I mean, I love the lights, I must be a bug or something, cause I'm always going after the lights. I remember the first time I stood on top of a hill and looked out over Baltimore, I said that's where I want to be. I have books in me. In the courtroom, I heard the judge talking about an armed, career-criminal, and I looked around to see who else was there. Me? I'm a good guy. Now I got time, I know I did the crime. If I ever get outta here, I know I won't write. I don't have the strength to deny myself outside. But I don't want to go back to what I did before, I'm not saying that. I know it was wrong. My novel's called *666 Pimpin*. Here's the synopsis. My characters are great. The ones you think are bad in the beginning turn out to be good and the ones you love turn out to be evil. It's 459 pages and it's a good read. Maybe your daughter would be interested—find out how not to be a prostitute. Nobody wants to talk about human trafficking, but it's everywhere. Let me explain. I keep my drug friends separate from my gorilla pimp friends. A regular pimp, the ladies be like, "Honey, I love you. You take care of me, and I'll give you all my money." Regular pimps got rules. A gorilla pimp be like he see a girl on the street, he tell her, "Woman, now you work for me." Take her? No, I don't take her. I just borrow her.

Definition according to *The Urban Dictionary*:
"Someone that pimps hoes through brute force. Uses excessive head twisting and arm breaking. As opposed to proper pimping through finesse, not force."
Example: *"That nigga a gorilla pimp, that's why his bitches look rough and beat up."*
https://www.urbandictionary.com/define.php?term=Gorilla%20Pimp

II: Writing Teacher

That's great that you call your cell a classroom, but I didn't hear you mention any authors who've inspired you to become a writer. Still, you show incredible dedication to your work by ignoring the TV in your cell and staying away from the Game-Boy. And, oh, I wish I could say how I feel about you giving your hard-earned $500 to that rip-off self-publishing company. I know, I know, you wanted to get the book out there, and they promised to promote it all over the internet—but they're only giving you 3 copies. And do you even get royalties? Still, when I hear the pride of accomplishment in your voice, I nod and smile. I have so many questions. Like, is your book a warning or a brag? Part of me hears the desire to caution people about how easy it is to get sucked into human trafficking, and I can't put my finger on it, but another part of me is chilled by your allusions to your past life. You're the only man in this prison who ever told me what he's in for. I never ask. How exactly are you using the word *pimpin'* in your title? And I won't ask you these questions in front of the other men, but one day, if it's just you and me in the writing group, here's what I'd say: *What happened to that young man who found a short-cut through the cemetery to his girlfriend's house? What happened to the kid who stole flowers from the grave sites and gave them to the girl and her mother? And what made him turn from cleaning up graves to selling drugs and then selling women?*

CPSIA information can be obtained
at www.ICGtesting.com
Printed in the USA
FSHW010111071021
85257FS